Dazzling
Disguises
and
Clever
Costumes

Angela Wilkes

Costumes by Jane Bull

DK

Dorling Kindersley, Inc.

LONDON, NEW YORK, MUNICH, MELBOURNE, and DELHI

Designer Adrienne Hutchinson
Assistant Designer Joanna Malivoire
Photographer Dave King
Editor Victoria Edgley
US Editor Camela Decaire
Jacket Designer Hedi Gutt
Jacket Editor Mariza O'Keeffe
Managing Editor Jane Yorke
Managing Art Editor Chris Scollen
Production Lucy Baker
DTP Designer Almudena Díaz

First American Edition, 1996

07 08 09 10 10 9 8 7 6 5 4 3
Published in the United States by
DK Publishing, Inc., 375 Hudson Street
New York, New York 10014
Copyright © 1996, 2006 Dorling Kindersley Limited, London
Text copyright © 1996 Angela Wilkes
First paperback edition 2006

A CIP catalog record is available from the Library of Congress.

Paperback edition ISBN 13: 978-0-7566-1935-0

Color reproduction by Bright Arts, Hong Kong
Printed and bound in China by Hung Hing Printing Co. Ltd.

DK would like to thank Adrienne Hutchinson and Joanna Malivoire for creating additional costumes, John Hutchinson for glasses template, Andy Crawford for additional photography and Carey Combe, Anne Marie Ryan, and Dean Price for their help in producing this book. DK would also like to thank the following models for appearing in this book: Ellisha Akhtar, Montana Burrett-Manning, Micheal Busby, Olivia Busby, Samantha Cobb, Holly Cowgill, Lawrence King, Sam King, Taskin Kuyucuoglu, Tolga Kuyucuoglu, Kim Ng, Sam Priddy, Tabedge

CONTENTS

MASKS AND HEADDRESSES

INTRODUCTION

This book is full of inspiring ideas to help you create a wide range of fantastic costumes and disguises from everyday materials. Below you can see some of the different materials that will come in handy. Collect as many of them as you can. It helps to keep them sorted into boxes, ready for some amazing transformations! When you finish a project, remember to put everything away and clean up any mess you have made.

Things to collect

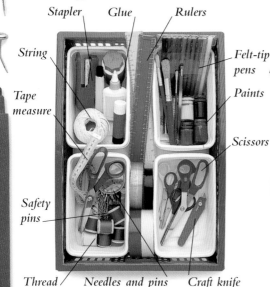

Stapler · Glue · Rulers · Felt-tip pens · Paints · Scissors · String · Tape measure · Safety pins · Thread · Needles and pins · Craft knife

Long-sleeved shirt · T-shirt · Vest

Bag · Beads · Belt · Hat · Ribbons · Scarves

Basic equipment

Collect as many craft and sewing materials as you can. You will need sharp scissors, colored thread, and different types of glue for cardboard and fabrics.

Old clothes

Keep old clothes and look for interesting items in second-hand stores. If the clothes are too big, you can easily cut them to fit.

Accessories

You can transform a costume with simple accessories. Collect bags, beads, belts, scarves, shoes, old glasses, and colored ribbons.

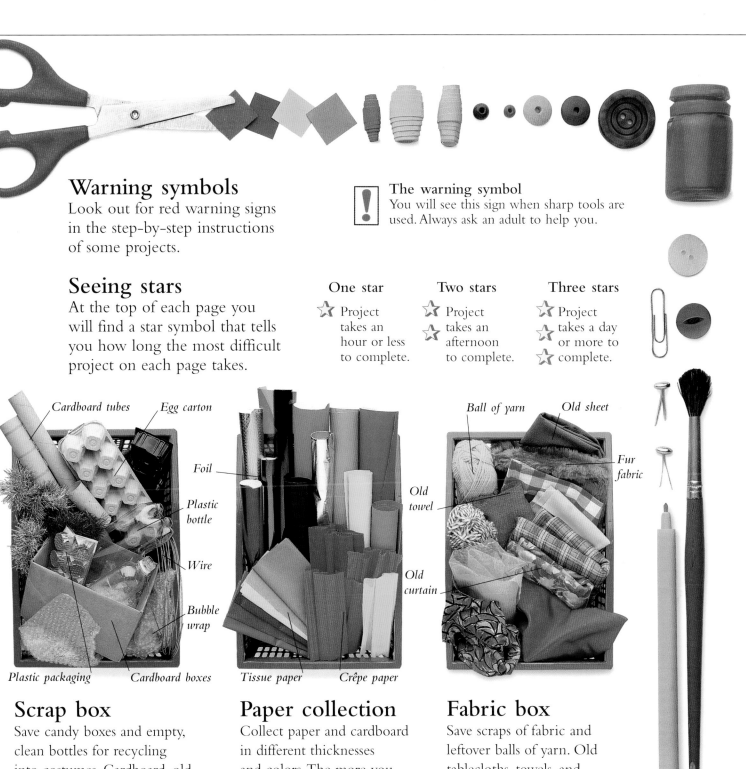

Warning symbols

Look out for red warning signs in the step-by-step instructions of some projects.

The warning symbol
You will see this sign when sharp tools are used. Always ask an adult to help you.

Seeing stars

At the top of each page you will find a star symbol that tells you how long the most difficult project on each page takes.

One star
☆ Project takes an hour or less to complete.

Two stars
☆ Project takes an afternoon to complete.

Three stars
☆ Project takes a day or more to complete.

Cardboard tubes

Egg carton

Foil

Plastic bottle

Wire

Bubble wrap

Plastic packaging

Cardboard boxes

Ball of yarn

Old sheet

Old towel

Fur fabric

Old curtain

Tissue paper

Crêpe paper

Scrap box

Save candy boxes and empty, clean bottles for recycling into costumes. Cardboard, old decorations, and plastic lids are all very useful.

Paper collection

Collect paper and cardboard in different thicknesses and colors. The more you have, the better. Try to find some foil paper and colored cellophane.

Fabric box

Save scraps of fabric and leftover balls of yarn. Old tablecloths, towels, and sheets are useful, and so are old curtains.

BOX MASKS

Here and on the next page you can find out how to make amazing lion, bird, and insect masks out of cardboard boxes. For each mask you will need a strong, light box that fits over your head as far as your shoulders. Below you can see how to make the boxes fit you so they won't slip when you have them on.

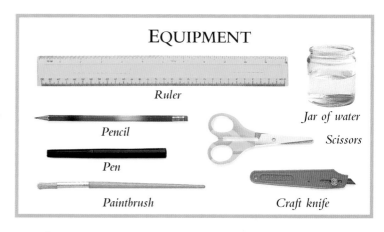

EQUIPMENT

Ruler

Pencil

Pen

Paintbrush

Jar of water

Scissors

Craft knife

You will need

Colored paper

Strong glue

Glue stick

Masking tape

Pieces of packaging

Clear tape

Colored tissue paper

Paint

Cardboard boxes

The basic box mask

1 Cut the flaps off a box (keep one flap for the lion mask). If the box is too long from front to back, cut it in half, as shown.

2 Slide one half of the box over the other until the box fits your head. Firmly tape the two halves together where they overlap.

3 Try the box on and feel where the eyeholes should be. Have someone mark the spots with a pencil. Take the box off and cut out eyeholes.

Wild lion

1 Leave one flap on the box. Cover the flap and front of the box, half of the top, and the sides with yellow paper, folding it and gluing it in place.

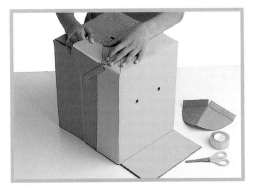

2 Cut out two cardboard ears and fold them in half. Cut a .5-in (1.5-cm) slit in the base and bend back tabs, as shown. Tape the tabs in place.

3 Tear up some short and long strips of orange and brown paper. Glue them to the front flap, top, and sides of the box to make a mane.

4 Tear out pieces of colored paper to make a nose, eyes, and whiskers. Glue them to the box and then draw on a mouth.

Exotic bird

1 Cover the back, top, and sides of a box with blue paper. Draw a bird's crest on cardboard, cut it out, and cover it with yellow paper.

2 Make .5-in (1.5-cm) cuts along the bottom of the crest. Fold each section back, alternating sides, to make tabs. Tape the tabs in place.

3 For a beak, cut out two cardboard triangles, one longer than the other. Cover them with yellow paper, fold in half, and bend tabs at the ends.

4 Tape the beak tabs to the front of the box. Gather several pieces of blue and lilac tissue paper and tear out feather shapes.

5 Glue the paper feathers to the box, working forward from the blue paper. Glue two circles of pink tissue paper around the eyeholes.

MASQUERADE

Evil insect

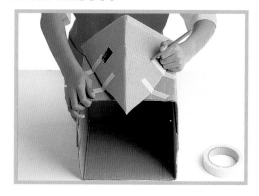

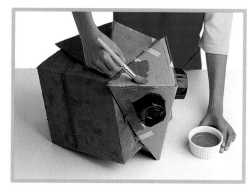

1 Cut three triangular corners of varying sizes off a box. Tape the largest one to the front of the box mask. Cut holes in it over the eyeholes.

2 Tape another corner to the top of the box and the last corner to the back. You may need to weight the back to balance the mask.

3 Stick pieces of plastic packaging over each eyehole and cut holes in them. Paint the whole mask with thick green paint and let it dry.

Wild lion
The mane for the lion mask is built up by gluing on long strips of paper first, then shorter strips just below the face.

Evil insect
You can vary the insect mask depending on the pieces of packaging you have at home. Anything black or shiny will do. Foil candy cups were used to give this bug its finishing touches.

Fur markings and other features are torn out of colored paper.

The mouth is drawn on with a thick black pen.

Antennae are made from strips of poster board with foil candy cups taped to the ends.

Glue torn strips of black paper around the mouth for whiskers.

4 Cut out circles of green foil and stick them onto the box. Glue the base of a green plastic bottle to the top of the box mask.

5 Cut three long strips of shiny poster board. Cut slits in the mask, slot the strips through, and tape them down to make antennae.

Birds and beasts

With a little imagination, each mask can be the basis for a whole costume. Turn to page 44 for some more ideas.

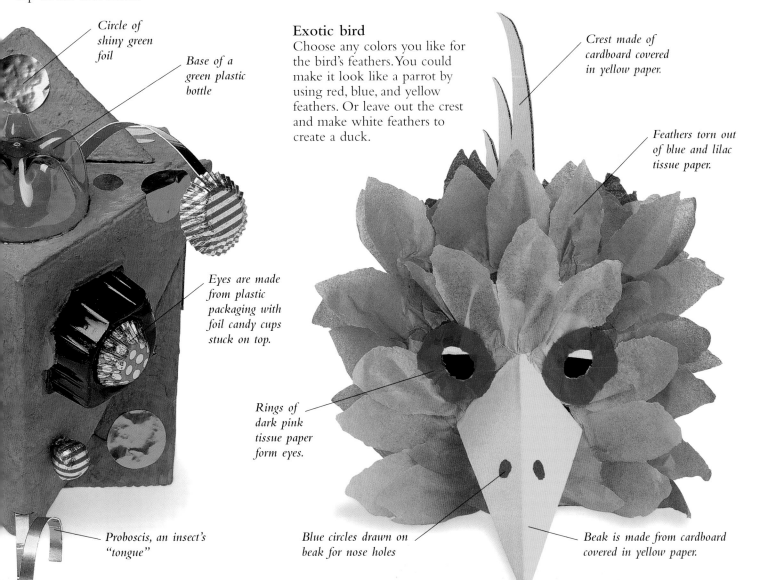

Circle of shiny green foil

Base of a green plastic bottle

Exotic bird
Choose any colors you like for the bird's feathers. You could make it look like a parrot by using red, blue, and yellow feathers. Or leave out the crest and make white feathers to create a duck.

Crest made of cardboard covered in yellow paper.

Feathers torn out of blue and lilac tissue paper.

Eyes are made from plastic packaging with foil candy cups stuck on top.

Rings of dark pink tissue paper form eyes.

Proboscis, an insect's "tongue"

Blue circles drawn on beak for nose holes

Beak is made from cardboard covered in yellow paper.

9

WILD STALLION

Gallop around with a friend in this fun costume for two. The horse is made in two pieces; a box mask for the head, and a fabric body. You can use fur fabric for the body, or perhaps an old blanket or towel.★ Turn the page to find out how to put the costume on together. You'll have to practice moving around in your finished horse, too.

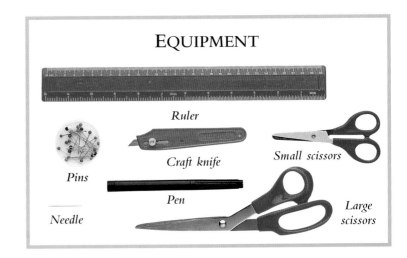

EQUIPMENT

Ruler

Pins

Craft knife

Small scissors

Needle

Pen

Large scissors

You will need

2 boxes each the same size, and big enough to fit over your head

3 sheets of brown paper

Glue

Clear tape

Black paper

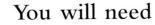

2 sheets of black crêpe paper

Spool of brown thread

Brown fur fabric 64 x 47 in

Dark brown, yellow, and white paper

Making the head

1 Cut off an end from one of the boxes. Slide the open end of the box inside the other box at right angles. Tape the two boxes together.

2 Cut along each side of the end of the outside box for a flap. Trim the boxes along the line shown. Cut the piece between the flap and line.

3 Draw and cut out two large ears on the leftover box pieces. Score a line down the middle of each ear with your scissors and fold the ears in half.

4 Cover the backs of the ears with brown paper and the insides with white and brown paper. Tape the ears to the top back corners of the head.

5 To cover the horse's head, cut out brown paper to fit the front, top, back, and sides of the box. Glue it in place with the glue stick.

6 Cut two nostril holes at the front of the head for your eyeholes.★ Glue on pieces of white and yellow paper for a blaze, eyes, and a mouth.

7 To make the mane, fold one sheet of black crêpe paper to a width of 7 in (18 cm). Cut strips into the folds, stopping 1 in (2 cm) from the top.

8 Open out the mane and glue it down the middle of the back of the head and neck. Make sure you leave a piece of mane for the forelock.

9 Fold up the black crêpe-paper forelock to fit the space between the horse's ears. Then carefully glue it in place.

Making the body

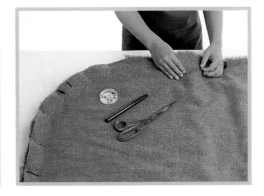

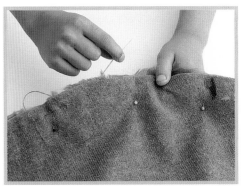

1 Fold the fabric in half lengthwise, fur side in, to make a rectangle 32 x 47 in (120 x 80 cm). Place the fold to your right.

2 Cut a curve in the top left-hand corner. Pin★ the fabric 12 in (30 cm) from the fold at the top and stop 14 in (36 cm) from the bottom edge.

3 Sew along the edges you have pinned, leaving a 2 in (5 cm) hole for the horse's tail marked on the curve. Turn the fabric fur side out.

HORSING AROUND

Making the tail

Making the hooves

1 Use a folded sheet of crêpe paper. Cut narrow strips along it, as you did for the mane, stopping 1.5 in (4 cm) from the top of the paper.

2 Bunch the tail together and wind clear tape around the top. Push the top into the hole in the body and secure it in place with tape.

Draw and cut four shapes out of black poster board as shown. Bend the strips until they fit neatly around your feet. Fasten the edges with tape.

Ready to gallop!

It takes some practice for two people to move around in a horse costume. Don't forget that the person at the back can't see where the horse is going, so walk together slowly before trying to gallop.

Changing places

The person at the back of the horse can get hot under the furry body, plus it's hard to stay bent over, so switch places often.

Horse head mask

Fur fabric body

Neck flap covered with crêpe-paper mane

Crêpe-paper tail

Putting on the costume

1 Put on the hooves. The front person puts his or her head through the neck hole of the body, and then puts the mask on.

2 The other person lifts the body up at the back, ready to duck inside. Make sure that the tail is untangled.

3 The back person should bend over and pull the back of the horse costume down, then put his or hers arms around the front person.

Zippy zebra
You can make a zebra costume in the same way as the horse – just use black and white fur fabric for the body and paper for the mask.

It is a good idea for both people to wear matching leggings or pants.

Bend the hooves around your feet and fasten the edges together at the back with tape.

Playtime
As part of a show, you can really make the audience laugh in a horse costume. Try dancing to music and hopping from one foot to another. End your show by curtseying with both pairs of legs. Try not to fall over!

White, brown, and black paper eyes

13

HATTER'S WORKSHOP

If you want to create a costume with just one item, make a hat. Tall hats, broad hats, pointed hats, or puffy hats – you can make anything following the simple methods shown here for cylinder, headband, and cone hats. Turn the page to find out how to decorate the hats and to see the stunning results.

EQUIPMENT

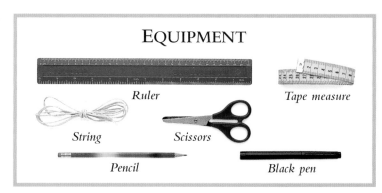

Ruler   Tape measure

String   Scissors

Pencil   Black pen

You will need

Poster board

Colored foil

Colored
tissue paper

Colored foil

Silky scarf

Glue stick

Cotton wool

Clear tape   Narrow
elastic

Strong glue

Colored
ribbons

Red tinsel

Headband hats

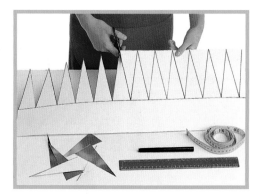

1 Measure around your head. Cut out a strip of poster board 1 in (3 cm) longer than the measurement. Tape the overlapping ends together.

2 To decorate the headband, draw shapes, such as leaves or stars, on the poster board. Cut them out and glue them to the headband.

3 For a crown, cut a headband 8.5 in (22 cm) deep out of gold poster board. Cut points halfway down the strip and tape the ends together.

Cylinder hat

1 Measure and cut out a rectangle of poster board as for a headband, but make it 6.5 in (17 cm) tall. Bend it into a cylinder and tape it.

2 Stand the cylinder in the middle of a piece of poster board and tape it in place. Draw a circle around it on the board, then untape it.

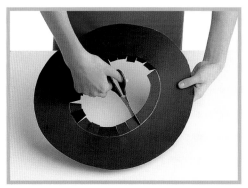

3 Draw a circle 3 in (7 cm) outside the first circle and cut around it. Cut out a circle 1 in (3 cm) inside the circle to make a brim, then cut tabs.

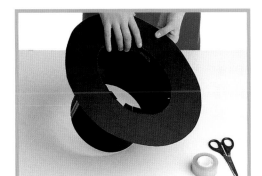

4 Fold the tabs up along the circle line. Place the cylinder over the tabs and tape them in place. Make sure that the brim sits straight.

Chef's hat

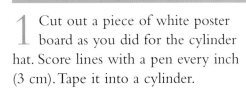

1 Cut out a piece of white poster board as you did for the cylinder hat. Score lines with a pen every inch (3 cm). Tape it into a cylinder.

2 Cut out a circle of tissue paper larger than the hat and tape pleats around the edge until it fits inside the top of the hat. Then tape it in place.

Cone hats

1 For tall hats, draw a quarter circle on poster board with a pencil tied to the end of a piece of string. Make the string the height you want the hat.

2 Cut out the hat along the line you have drawn. For shorter hats, you will need to draw and cut out a half-circle.

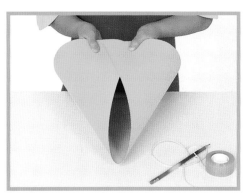

3 Roll the quarter circle into a cone, then try it on your head and adjust it until it fits you. Tape the two straight edges together.

HATS ON PARADE

Starry witch

1 To make the notched brim for a witch's hat, cut tabs about 1 in (3 cm) deep all the way around the bottom of the cone. Fold the tabs up.

2 To add the finishing touches to the witch's hat, cut out stars and diamonds from shiny green paper and glue them to the hat and brim.

Regal crown

Glue foil candy cups around the crown to make jewels. Stick cotton around the base of the crown and add tiny pieces of black paper.

Medieval lady's hat

1 Cut a hole on each side of a tall cone hat. Thread elastic through the holes to make a chin strap. Secure each end with a knot.

2 Tape colored ribbons from top to bottom of the cone hat. Then attach a folded piece of tissue paper around the bottom.

Hat collection

Here you can see the basic headband, cylinder, and cone hat shapes transformed into wreaths, crowns, and top hats. See how many more hats you can invent using these basic shapes.

Silky scarf

Clown hat
This small cone hat is made from yellow poster board and decorated with red paper spots and tinsel.

Emperor's wreath
Based on a Roman emperor's wreath, this headband is decorated with ivy leaves cut out of metallic gold poster board.

Witch's hat
This cone hat has a notched brim and is decorated with foil stars. You could make a wizard's cone hat from dark blue paper and silver stars.

Magician's top hat
The magician's hat has a narrow brim and a band of red ribbon around the cylinder. Tuck a toy bunny in the top for an added surprise.

Tall cylinder

Notched brim

Chef's hat
The chef's hat is made from scored white poster board taped into a cylinder. A puff of white tissue paper forms the crown.

Regal crown
Decorate a gold crown made from a headband with cotton, construction paper, and foil candy cups.

Folded tissue paper taped to the brim

Large brim

Narrow red ribbon

Medieval lady's hat
This tall cone hat has stripes made from narrow, colored ribbons and a floaty scarf taped to the top.

Matador's hat
A short cylinder hat with a very wide brim gives this black paper hat its matador shape.

SPACE-AGE ROBOT

To create your own robot costume, look for interesting pieces of packaging around your home. The key piece is the helmet. You will need something big enough to cover most of your head. We used a popcorn carton painted blue, but you could use a box, or make an upside-down hat out of poster board (see p.14-15). Use bright colors to create a friendly robot, or try using black and silver to for a scary robot.

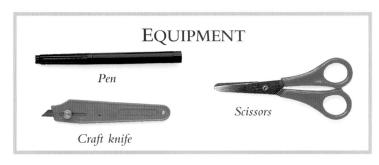

EQUIPMENT

Pen

Scissors

Craft knife

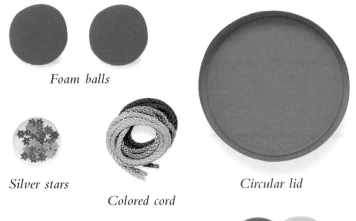

Foam balls

Silver stars

Colored cord

Circular lid

You will need

T-shirt

A round carton

Pipe cleaners

Glue

Poster board

Bottle tops

Making the helmet

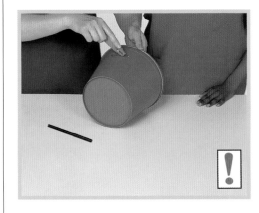

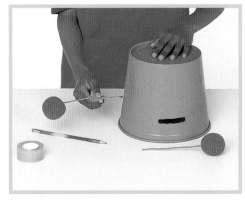

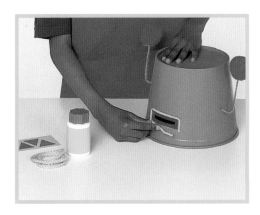

1 Try the carton on your head and have someone mark where the eyeholes shuold be. Cut a long rectangular slot around the marks.

2 Stick foam balls on the ends of two pipe cleaners. Make two tiny holes in the sides of the carton and push the pipe cleaners into them.

3 Bend the pipe cleaners upward. Decorate the carton with shapes of colored poster board and glue pipe cleaners around the eye-slot.

Decorating the T-shirt

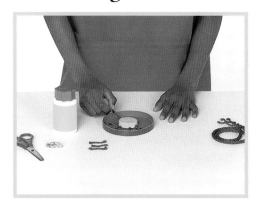

1 Paint the circular lid bright colors and glue a bottle top in the middle of it. Glue short pieces of cord inside the lid, as shown.

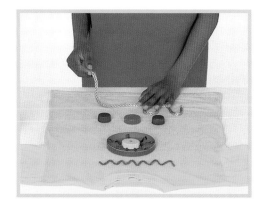

2 Glue the lid to the center of the T-shirt to look like a control panel. Glue down bottle tops and wiggly lines of cord for decoration.

Robot power

The helmet and T-shirt give you the basis for your robot costume. Turn to page 44 for ideas of more things to add to your outfit. Don't forget to move your arms and legs stiffly, like a robot!

Robot head
The finished helmet provides a complete disguise because it covers your face – no one will be able to see your eyes. The wobbly antennae will pick up any robot radar messages!

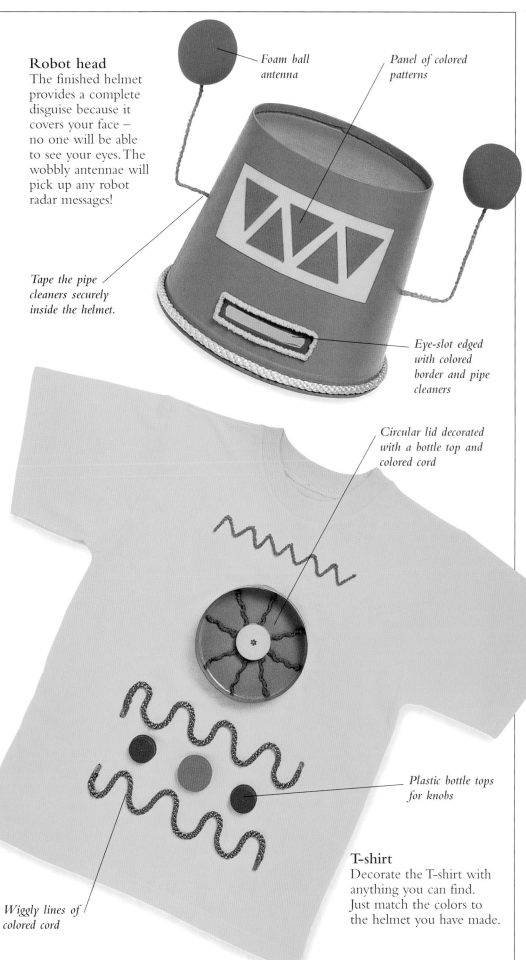

Foam ball antenna

Panel of colored patterns

Tape the pipe cleaners securely inside the helmet.

Eye-slot edged with colored border and pipe cleaners

Circular lid decorated with a bottle top and colored cord

Plastic bottle tops for knobs

Wiggly lines of colored cord

T-shirt
Decorate the T-shirt with anything you can find. Just match the colors to the helmet you have made.

GHOSTS AND HORRORS

It's Halloween night. It's dark outside, ghouls and goblins are all around, and you want to join in the ghostly fun. Or maybe you just want to give your friends a terrifying scare. Here you can find out how to use an old sheet or pillowcase★ to transform yourself into a ghoulish ghost or a grizzly mummy that look like they've just stepped out of a horror movie.

EQUIPMENT

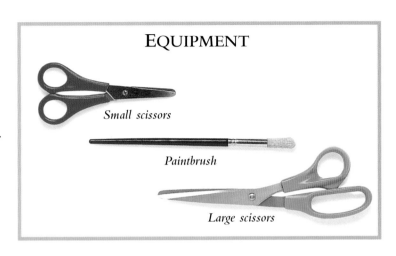

Small scissors

Paintbrush

Large scissors

You will need

Large white sheet, tablecloth, or piece of fabric

Black felt

Glue   *Colored tape*

Ghoulish ghost

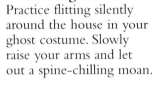

1 Put the sheet on and mark where the eyeholes should be with tape. Take the sheet off. Cut out felt eyes and glue them over the tape.

2 Cut out a felt mouth and glue it below the eyes. Then pinch each felt eye and cut a small hole in the middle of it.

Ghoulish ghost

Practice flitting silently around the house in your ghost costume. Slowly raise your arms and let out a spine-chilling moan.

Black felt eyes

Black felt mouth

Trim the bottom of the sheet so that it is straight.

3 Put the sheet on again, with the eyeholes in the right place. Ask an adult to trim around the bottom of the sheet to make a straight hem.

Horror mummy

You will need

White pillowcase

Torn strips of a white sheet or cotton fabric

Colored tape

Red paint

1 Put the pillowcase on and mark the position of your face with tape. Take the pillowcase off, cut a face hole, and then trim off the bottom.

2 Put the pillowcase back on. Ask a friend to loosely wind strips of fabric around your head to hold the pillowcase in place.

Finishing touches

Ask your friend to paint a red "wound" on the side of your head. Then bend one arm across your stomach so it can be bandaged up. You can also bandage your free arm and hand.

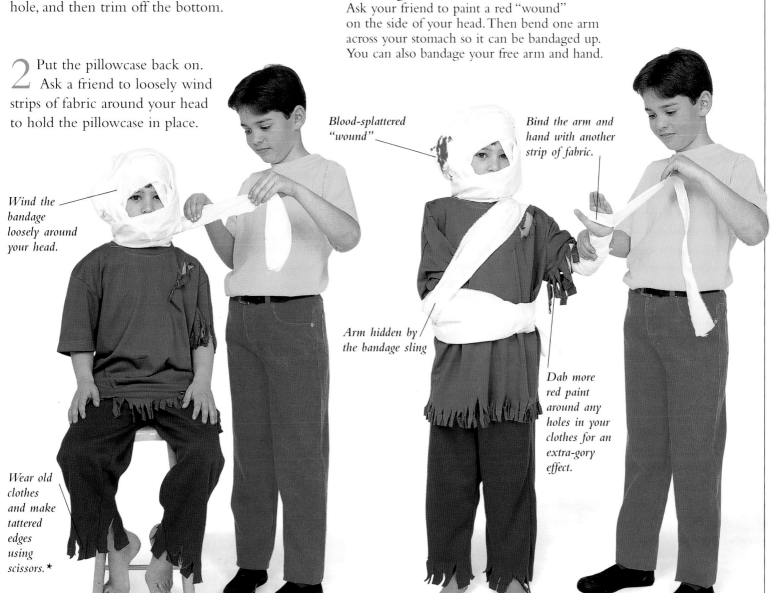

Wind the bandage loosely around your head.

Wear old clothes and make tattered edges using scissors. ★

Blood-splattered "wound"

Arm hidden by the bandage sling

Bind the arm and hand with another strip of fabric.

Dab more red paint around any holes in your clothes for an extra-gory effect.

UNDER WRAPS

Some costumes are very simple to make and can be invented by playing around with whatever odds and ends of fabric you have, such as old towels, sheets, or tablecloths.★ You wrap, twist, tug, and tie – and instantly you are a Roman emperor or a desert island dancer! Big safety pins are handy for these costumes, and ribbons, jewelry, and flowers are great accessories.

EQUIPMENT

Pinking shears

Tape measure

Large scissors

You will need

For a sarong

A piece of flowery fabric about 35 x 65 in (90 x 170 cm)

Smaller piece of same fabric about 12 x 65 in (170 x 30 cm)

Crêpe-paper flower

The skirt needs to be pulled tightly around your waist.

Paper flower in hair

The material is tied together at the back of the neck.

Narrow piece of fabric

Tie the fabric in a knot at the side.

Sarong

Place the narrow piece of fabric around your back. Then cross the ends of the fabric over your chest and tie them behind your neck. Wrap the large piece of fabric around your waist and tie the ends together at the side.

Arrange the fabric so that it falls in folds.

Start wrapping

Here you can see how to make an exotic sarong, a Roman toga, and a regal turban. All of the costumes are made simply by wrapping pieces of fabric around your body and fastening them in place.

You will need

For a Roman toga

Safety pins

*Pin and belt
(see page 42)*

Gold ribbon or cord

2 large white towels

*Emperor's wreath
(see page 14)*

Roman toga

Wrap one towel tightly around your waist like a skirt. Tuck in the ends and pin them securely. Drape the second towel over one shoulder and tuck the front into the skirt.

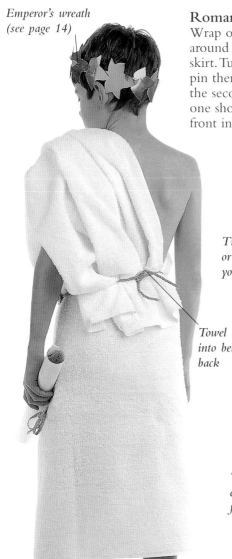

Gather the towel in with cord and fasten on a pin.

Tie a belt, ribbon, or cord around your waist.

Towel tucked into belt at the back

Towel folds over at the front.

Paper scroll

You will need

For a turban

A long piece of silky fabric

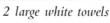

*Pin
(see page 42)*

Twist the ends of the fabric together tightly, as shown.

Turban

Wrap the fabric around your head with the ends in front. Twist the ends together, flip them back over the turban, and tuck them in at the back of your head.

Decorate the front of the turban with a pin.

23

TUNICS

A tunic makes a great base for any costume. It is simple to make, and it can be dressed up by adding belts, scarves, jewelry, or anything else you have around the house. Here you can see how to make a royal tunic and a forest archer tunic without doing any sewing at all. You can use any type of fabric, and vary your costume with colors and patterns.

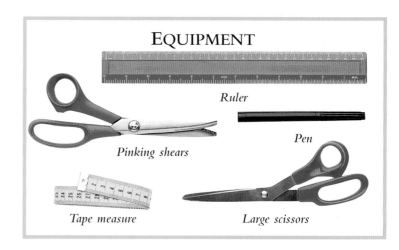

EQUIPMENT

Ruler

Pinking shears

Pen

Tape measure

Large scissors

You will need

For the archer tunic

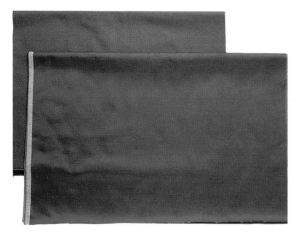

28 x 55 in (140 x 70 cm) fabric for each tunic

Pouch made from circle of fabric tied with cord

Narrow scarf or belt

For the royal tunic

Medallion (see page 42)

Necklace or chain (see page 42)

Wide gold ribbon or cord

Royal tunic

1 Lay the fabric out flat on a table or the floor, smoothing out any wrinkles. Measure and cut out a piece 28 x 55 in (140 x 70 cm) wide.

2 Fold the fabric in half lengthwise. Measure 6 in (15 cm) in from each edge on the fold. Cut a slit between the marks as a neck hole.

3 Using the pinking shears, trim 0.25 in (0.5 cm) along all the outer edges of the tunic. This will help stop the fabric from fraying.

Archer tunic

1 Follow steps 1 and 2 for the royal tunic. Then cut a slit 6 in (15 cm) long in the center front of the neck to make the collar flaps.

2 Draw deep points along the bottom edges of the tunic using a ruler and pen. Cut along the lines you have drawn to make a ragged edge.

Tunic outfits

These two tunics can be worn over T-shirts or on their own. Tie a scarf, ribbon, or cord belt around your waist or hips and add other decorations to fit the character you are playing. You can vary the basic tunic by making it in different fabrics, or by cutting out a larger piece of material and turning it into a dress.

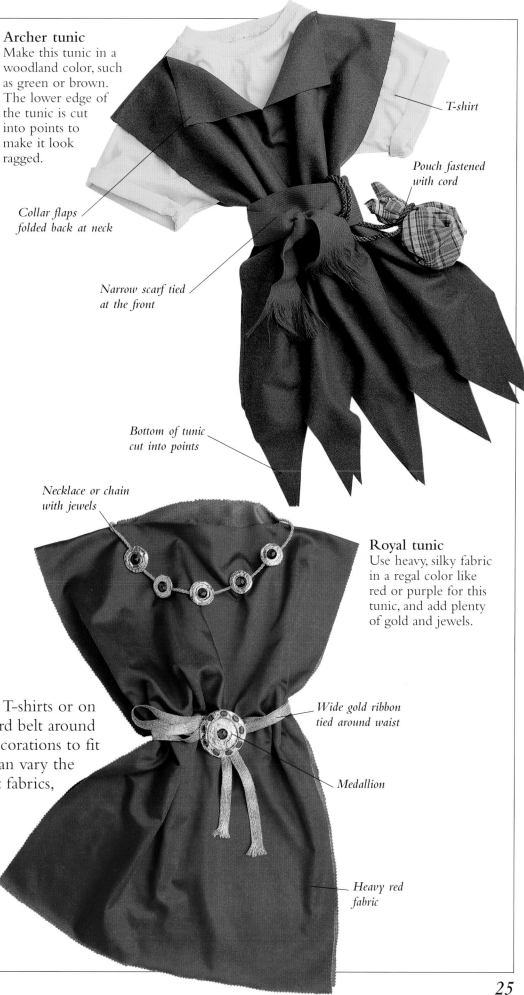

Archer tunic
Make this tunic in a woodland color, such as green or brown. The lower edge of the tunic is cut into points to make it look ragged.

T-shirt

Pouch fastened with cord

Collar flaps folded back at neck

Narrow scarf tied at the front

Bottom of tunic cut into points

Necklace or chain with jewels

Royal tunic
Use heavy, silky fabric in a regal color like red or purple for this tunic, and add plenty of gold and jewels.

Wide gold ribbon tied around waist

Medallion

Heavy red fabric

TATTERED SKIRTS

You don't need to be a whiz with a needle and thread to make your own costumes. Here you can find out how to make a stunning range of grass skirts using colored crêpe paper. You can follow the ideas on this page or design your own variations.

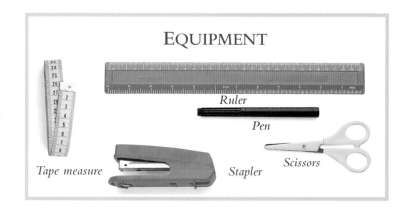

EQUIPMENT

Ruler

Pen

Tape measure   Stapler   Scissors

You will need

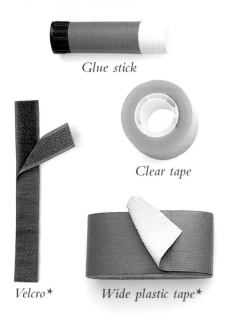

Glue stick

Clear tape

Velcro★   Wide plastic tape★

Colored crêpe paper

Basic grass skirt

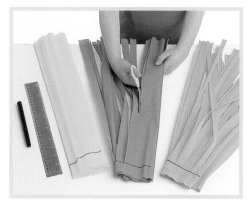

1 Measure around your waist with the tape measure and add 2 in (60 mm) to the measurement. Cut some wide plastic tape to the same length.

2 Cut three pieces of crêpe paper the same length as the tape. Fold and cut them into thin strips, stopping 1 in (25 mm) from the top.

3 Stick each piece of paper in layers to the lower half of the tape. Fold the top half of the tape down over them.

★Available from large department or arts and crafts stores.

Ra-ra skirt

Rags and tatters skirt

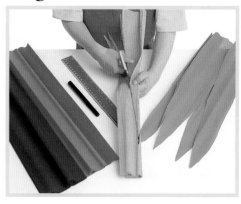

4 Cover the tape with crêpe paper and decorate it with paper shapes. Staple Velcro to each end of the skirt, for fastening it around you.

Make this in the same way as the grass skirt, but shorter. Attach seven or more layers of crêpe paper cut to different lengths to the tape.

Follow the basic grass skirt steps. Use five pieces of different-colored crêpe paper for this skirt, cutting the skirt strips into points.

Dancing skirts

Choose contrasting colors for your skirt so it will stand out. Turn to page 44 to see how to use these skirts as part of a costume.

Waistband decorated with triangles of crêpe paper

Ra-ra skirt
Layered crêpe paper gives this skirt a ruffled appearance.

Grass skirt
This skirt is made up of one layer each of yellow, orange, and green crêpe paper.

Rags and tatters skirt
The pointed strips give this skirt its ragged look.

CLOAKS AND CAPES

Swirling cloaks and capes are an important addition to many costumes. Kings, queens, witches, wizards, and even birds and insects look best with dramatic cloaks. Here you'll learn two easy methods for making cloaks, one for regal robes and the other for fluttering capes. Turn the page for more ideas.

EQUIPMENT

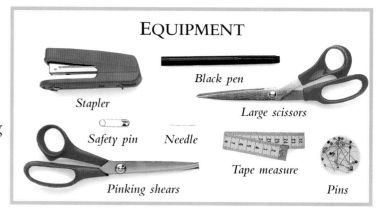

Stapler

Black pen

Large scissors

Safety pin   Needle

Tape measure

Pinking shears

Pins

You will need

For witch's cape

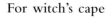

Colored foil

47 x 47 in (120 x 120 cm) black fabric

Wide gold ribbon

Green cellophane

For bird's wings

Roll of bubble wrap

Colored tissue paper

For regal robes

White fur fabric

Red thread

Wide red ribbon

Glue

Black paper

47 x 47 in (120 x 120 cm) red fabric

Bird wings

1 Tape together sheets of bubble wrap to make a piece 64 x 32 in (160 x 80 cm). Fold it into a square. Cut a neck hole and trim the bottom.

2 Draw and cut out points along the bottom edge of the cape. Cut two strips of bubble wrap for ties and staple one to each side of the neck.

3 Gather together colored tissue paper. Carefully tear out lots of feather shapes. You will need both large and small feathers.

4 Tape the larger feathers onto the cape in rows. Pinch each feather in the middle as you tape it down to make it stick out a little.

5 Tape over the staples attaching the neck ties to cover any sharp ends. Then decorate the neck edge with the smaller feathers.

6 Cut two long, narrow strips of bubble wrap. Bend them into loops and staple them to each side of the cape to make wrist loops.

Regal robe

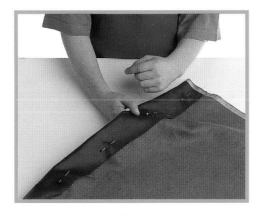

1 Trim the red fabric. Fold one edge of the fabric, 2 in (6 cm) wide, to the back side and pin it in place to make a casing for a ribbon.

2 Thread a needle with a double thread and knot it at the end. Sew firmly along the bottom edge of the folded fabric as shown.

3 With pinking shears, cut strips of fur fabric 2 in (6 cm) wide. Use these pieces of fabric to decorate the sides and bottom edges of the robe.

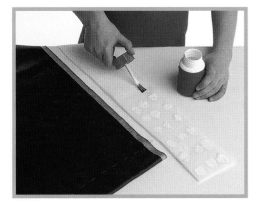

4 Dab glue along the back of each fur strip. Glue the strips of fur onto the front of the robe and down the sides and along the bottom edges.

5 Cut out lots of small rectangles of black paper. Carefully glue them all over the fur fabric on the robe, as shown.

6 Thread a long ribbon through the folded casing at the top of the robe using a safety pin. Gather the fabric as you pull the ribbon through.

CAPE COLLECTION

You can create your own costume by using different materials and unusual decorations to adapt the cloaks and capes shown here.

Feathers torn out of different-colored tissue paper

Pointed edges cut into the bubble wrap

Wrist loop

Bird's wings
Fasten the ties loosely around your neck and slip your hands through the wrist loops. Lift your arms and flap your wings!

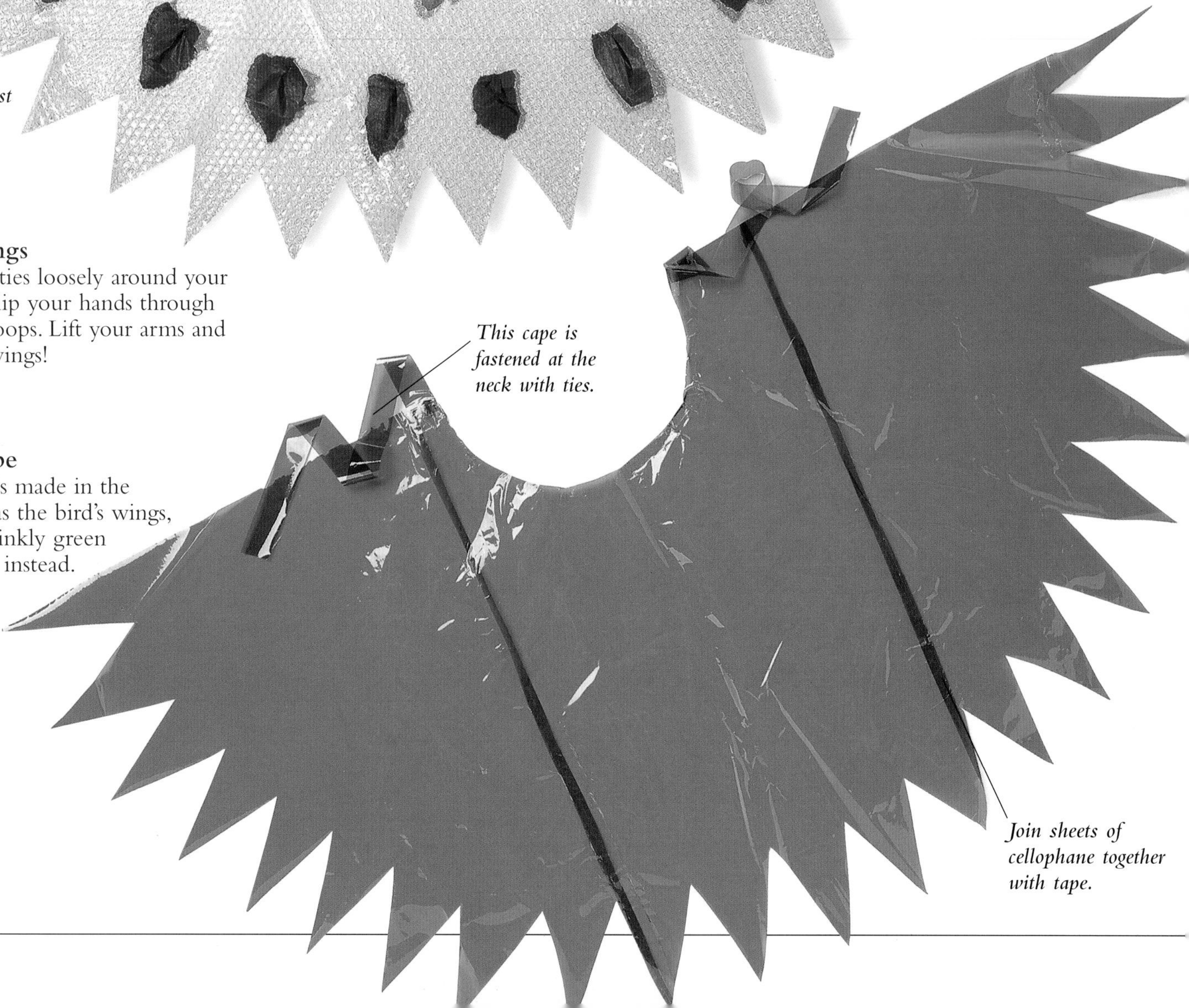

This cape is fastened at the neck with ties.

Insect cape
This cape is made in the same way as the bird's wings, but uses crinkly green cellophane instead.

Join sheets of cellophane together with tape.

Tie the neck ties in a loose bow.

Finishing touches

Here are just a few ideas for cloaks and capes. You could make a wizard's cape using blue material and green stars. Why not make the hat on page 14 to wear with the cape? Or the king's crown to wear with the regal robe? Turn to the Costume Parade on page 44 for even more ideas on what to wear with the wings and cloaks.

Broad ribbon gathers the cloak in at the neck.

Trim made from white fur fabric and pieces of black paper

Stars made from colored foil

Regal robe
Choose a dark red or purple fabric for this cloak to give it a truly royal appearance.

Witch's cape
To make this cape, follow the pattern for the regal robe, but use black material instead. Decorate it with silver and gold stars cut from foil and a gold ribbon.

MIGHTY WEAPONS

Here and on the next page you can see how to make a suit of shining armor, complete with a sword and a dagger worthy of the most valiant knight. Everything is made of corrugated cardboard from cardboard boxes and extra-wide aluminum foil. Before you make the breastplate, measure yourself and adapt the armor pattern to fit your body.

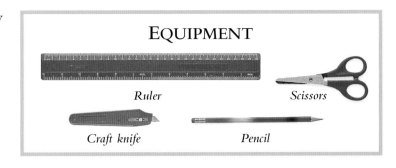

EQUIPMENT

Ruler   Scissors

Craft knife   Pencil

You will need

Glue stick   Strong glue   Clear tape

Extra-wide aluminum foil   Paper fasteners

Long and short cardboard tubes

Thick, corrugated cardboard   String   Black colored tape   Red colored tape   Colored paper

Making the breastplate

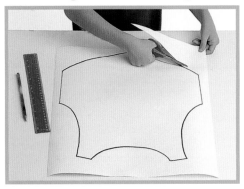

1 Draw a breastplate pattern on paper, with neck and armholes 8 in (20 cm) wide. The distance from neck to waist is 14.5 in (37 cm).

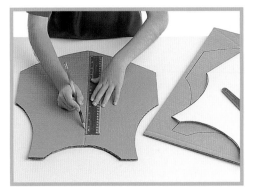

2 Using this pattern, draw and cut two breastplates out of corrugated cardboard. Score a line down the middle and fold each breastplate.

3 Cut two strips of cardboard 1.25 x 16 in (3.5 x 40 cm). Cover the strips and breastplates with foil, taping it in place at the back of each piece.

4 Make a hole in each shoulder of each breastplate. Attach the strips to the breastplates, using the holes, with paper fasteners.

5 Make three holes down the sides of each breastplate. Thread a long piece of string through the holes, just like you would thread a shoelace.

6 Decorate the front breastplate with paper fasteners as shown. Make a paper shield design and glue it to the middle of the breastplate.

Making the shield

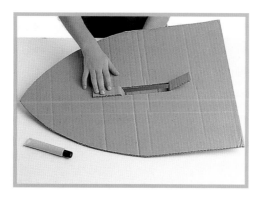

1 Cut two 20 x 16 in (50 x 40 cm) shields out of corrugated cardboard as shown. Cut a slot 5 x 1 in (12.5 x 3 cm) in the middle of one shield.

2 Cut out a strip 9 x 1.25 in 2.75 x 23 cm) of strong cardboard. Fold it to make a handle. Push it in the slot and glue the ends in place.

3 Glue the shields together, with the handle at the back. Seal the edges with tape. Decorate the shield with a colored paper design.

Making the helmet

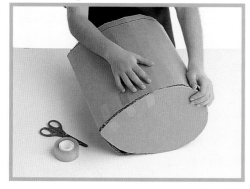

1 Cut out a cardboard rectangle 32 x 12 in (80 x 30 cm). Tape it into a pointed cylinder shape. Make a top for the helmet and tape it in place.

2 Try the helmet on. Then draw and cut out curves along the bottom edge of the helmet so that it sits comfortably on your shoulders.

3 Cut four slits in the front of the helmet for eyeholes. Cover the helmet with foil and decorate it with paper fasteners and a paper design.

ON GUARD!

Weapon blades

Flatten two cardboard tubes, one long and one short. Cut one end of each tube into a point. Tape the ends. Cover the tubes with foil, taping the join.

Dagger handle

Cut a cardboard rectangle 6.5 x 2.5 in (17 x 6 cm) with a slit in the center. Slide the short blade through the slit. Fold the handle in half and tape it.

Sword handle

Cut a piece of cardboard 13 x 3 in (34 x 8 cm) with rounded ends. Cover it with black tape. Cut two slits in each end as long as the sword is wide.

Finishing touches

Bend the sword handle as shown. Slide it over the top of the sword. Wrap tape around the blade to keep the handle in place. Decorate with colored tape.

Gauntlets

Cut two boat-shaped cardboard pieces wide enough to go around your wrists. Tape the ends together, then decorate with foil and paper fasteners.

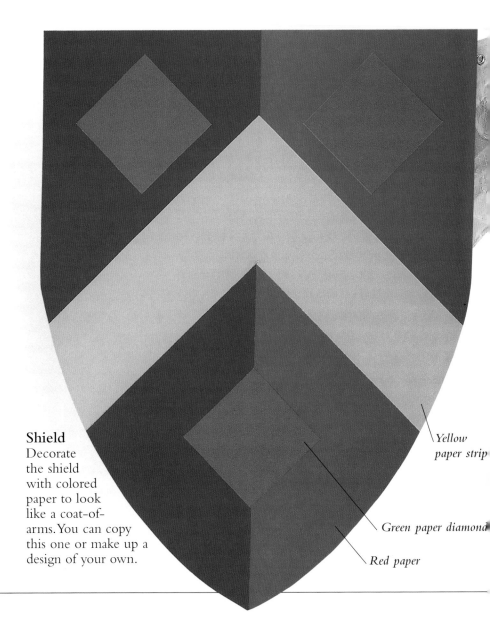

Shield
Decorate the shield with colored paper to look like a coat-of-arms. You can copy this one or make up a design of your own.

Yellow paper strip

Green paper diamond

Red paper

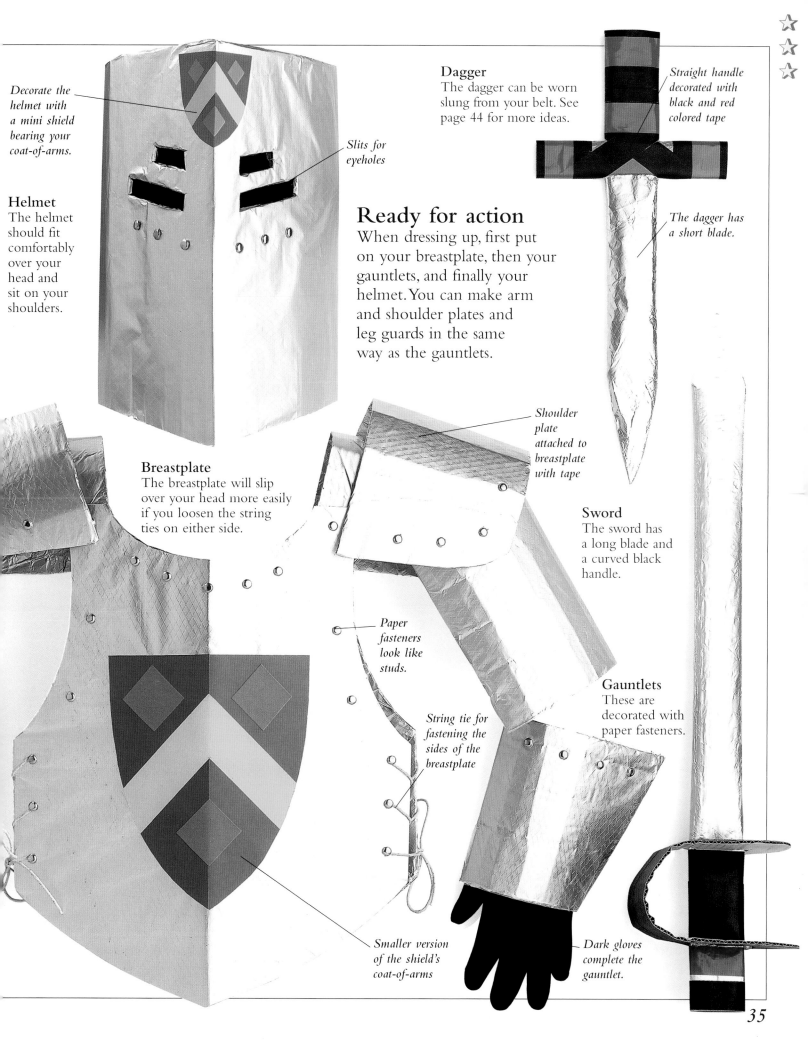

Decorate the helmet with a mini shield bearing your coat-of-arms.

Helmet
The helmet should fit comfortably over your head and sit on your shoulders.

Slits for eyeholes

Dagger
The dagger can be worn slung from your belt. See page 44 for more ideas.

Straight handle decorated with black and red colored tape

The dagger has a short blade.

Ready for action
When dressing up, first put on your breastplate, then your gauntlets, and finally your helmet. You can make arm and shoulder plates and leg guards in the same way as the gauntlets.

Shoulder plate attached to breastplate with tape

Breastplate
The breastplate will slip over your head more easily if you loosen the string ties on either side.

Sword
The sword has a long blade and a curved black handle.

Paper fasteners look like studs.

String tie for fastening the sides of the breastplate

Gauntlets
These are decorated with paper fasteners.

Smaller version of the shield's coat-of-arms

Dark gloves complete the gauntlet.

FIENDISH DEVIL

On the days you feel like being really devilish, this is the perfect costume. Like many successful costumes it relies on just a simply decorated T-shirt and a few cunning accessories for its effect; in this case curved horns and a pointed tail. You will need a really big T-shirt to decorate; it should be long enough to reach your thighs.

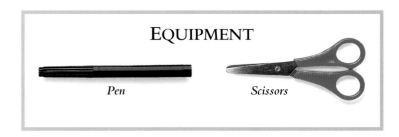

EQUIPMENT

Pen

Scissors

Red fabric

Glue

Wire

Safety pin

You will need

Orange and yellow felt

Red T-shirt

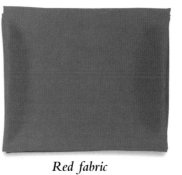

Red poster board

Headband

Decorating the T-shirt

1 Draw flame shapes on orange and yellow felt and cut them out. Make the orange flames smaller and narrower than the yellow ones.

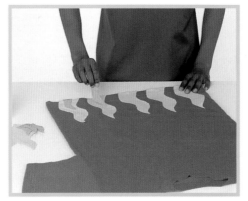

2 Glue the yellow flames along the bottom of the T-shirt, then glue the orange ones on top. Do the same with the sleeves and shoulders.

Horns

Draw two small, curved horns on red poster board and cut them out. Carefully glue them to the front of the headband as shown.

Pointed tail

1 Cut out a strip of fabric 40 x 4 in (100 x 10 cm). Fold the fabric in half lengthwise, right-side in. Glue the long edges together like a tube.

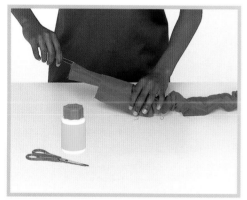

2 When the glue is dry, attach a safety pin to one end of the tail. Thread the pin through the tube to turn the fabric right-side out.

3 Thread 25 in (65 cm) of wire inside the tail. Cut two triangles and glue them together over one end of the tube. Glue the other end shut.

Feeling devilish

To complete the costume, attach the tail to the back of the T-shirt with a large safety pin and pull on a pair of red tights.

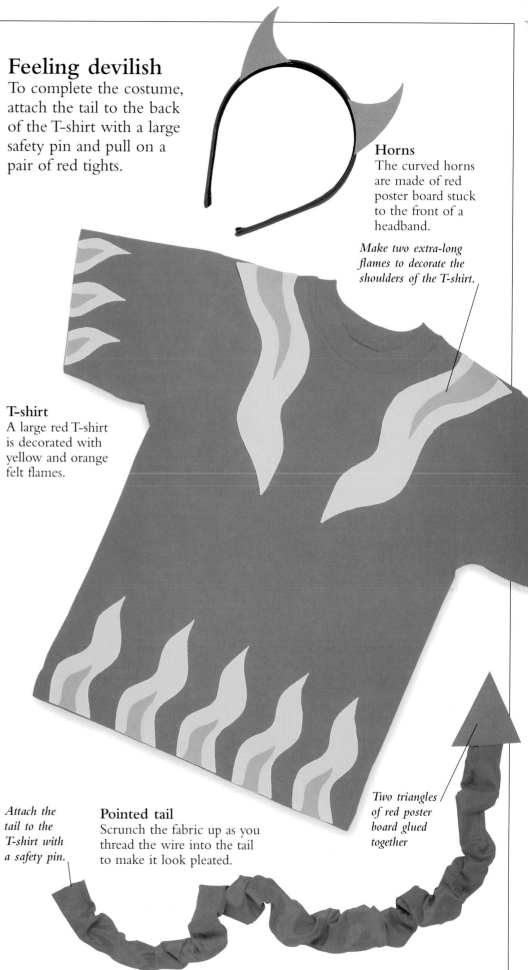

Horns
The curved horns are made of red poster board stuck to the front of a headband.

Make two extra-long flames to decorate the shoulders of the T-shirt.

T-shirt
A large red T-shirt is decorated with yellow and orange felt flames.

Two triangles of red poster board glued together

Attach the tail to the T-shirt with a safety pin.

Pointed tail
Scrunch the fabric up as you thread the wire into the tail to make it look pleated.

HAIRY DISGUISES

For a complete change of face, why not make yourself a bushy beard and bristling mustache? Or hide your own hair under a hat and grow some chunky braids? Here you can make both these hairy disguises, as well as a useful collection of false mustaches.

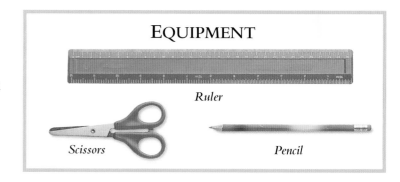

EQUIPMENT

Ruler

Scissors

Pencil

You will need

For the braids

Hat

Yarn   *Wire*   *Safety pins*   *Ribbon*

For the beard and mustache

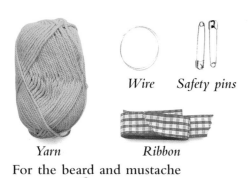

Yarn

Glue   *White poster board*   *Narrow elastic*

For paper mustaches

Black poster board

Paper mustache

Fold the black poster board in half. Draw half a mustache shape, as shown, next to the fold. Cut out the shape and then open out the mustache.

2 Cut pieces of yarn twice the length you want the beard. Loop 3 pieces of yarn at a time around the lower part of the mouth piece and tie.

Woolly beard

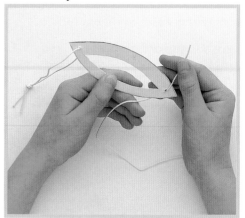

1 Cut out a mouth piece as shown. Make a small hole in each side, then thread a piece of elastic through each hole and tie it into a loop.

3 For the mustache, cut shorter lengths of yarn. Lay them across the top of the mouth piece and tie them in place with a piece of yarn.

Chunky braids

  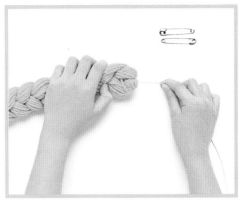

1 Cut 40 pieces of yarn the length you want each braid to be. Split the yarn into three bunches. Tie them firmly together at one end as shown.

2 Braid the yarn, starting from where it is tied together. Secure the end of the braid tightly, too, to stop it from unraveling.

3 Thread some wire through each braid. Pin the finished ends inside the hat with safety pins. Tie bows around the other ends of the braids.

Cover-ups

You can add other items, such as a hat, glasses, or scarf, to complete your disguise. Turn to page 44 for more costume ideas to wear with the mustaches, beards, and braids.

Long and pointed mustache

Curly mustache

Adapt the nose pieces to fit your nose.

Small mustache

Mustaches
The mustaches vary in shape but are all made from black poster board.

Wire in the braid lets you bend it into funny shapes.

Chunky braids
By using different-colored yarn or other hats, you can create a whole new costume.

Elastic loops

Gingham bow

Woolly beard
Hook the loops of elastic around your ears to keep the bushy beard and mustache in place.

SPECS AND SHADES

Spectacles make great instant disguises because they completely change the appearance of your face. You can become a glittering rock star or transform yourself into a pop-eyed mad professor. Trace the patterns below and transfer them onto cardboard to create a set of basic templates for making fantastic eyewear.

EQUIPMENT

Pencil   *Scissors*

Colored poster board

You will need

Colored sequins   *Clear tape*   *Narrow elastic*   *Glue*   *Felt-tip pens*   *Drinking straws*   *Tubes of glitter*   *Feathers*

Clear and colored acetate

Pieces of egg carton

Needle

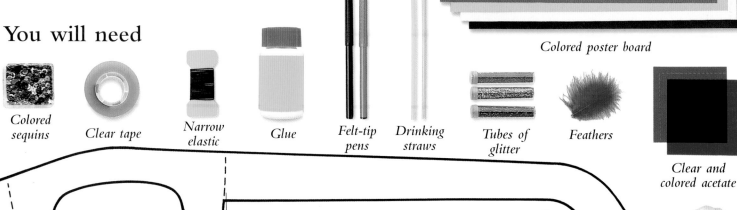

Nose

Eye patch pattern

Half pattern for basic glasses

Movie star

Basic glasses

1 Draw around the basic glasses template on black poster board. Carefully cut out the glasses and fold back the arms.

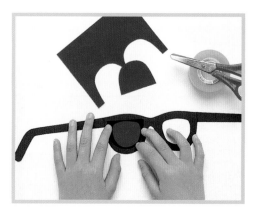

2 Cut out two pieces of colored acetate slightly larger than the eyeholes in the frames. Tape them in place on the back of the frames.

Eye patch

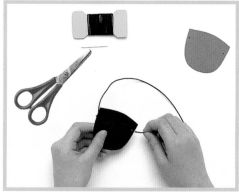

Draw and cut out a black poster board eye patch using the pattern. Make two holes in it. Thread some elastic through the holes and knot the ends.

Pop-out eyes

 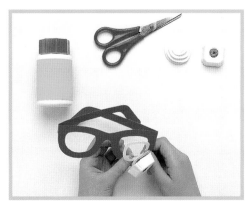

1 Make a pair of plain glasses with clear acetate lenses. Cut out two sections of egg carton and draw an eye on the top of each one.

2 Cut two spirals out of white poster board as shown. Glue one end of each spiral to the back of an eyeball and the other end to the lens.

Rock star shades

Add the wings to the template before drawing around it. Glue glitter and sequins to the frames and make lenses from colored acetate.

Red shades
Give your basic glasses red lenses to see things in a different light.

Red lenses   *Black frames*

Knotted end of elastic

Pirate's eye patch
Eye patches come in very handy for pirate costumes.

Glasses gallery
Decide what character you want to be and make your eyewear accordingly. Experiment with the shapes of the frames and use colored acetate to cunningly disguise the color of your eyes.

Masquerade
To make a party mask, draw around the glasses template without the arms. Cut out small eyeholes and decorate with colored paper, feathers, and sequins.

Feathers taped to outer edges

Tape the mask to a drinking straw.

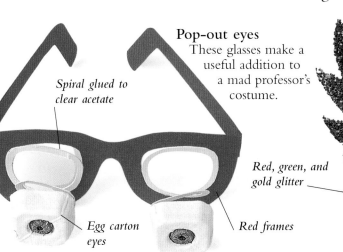

Pop-out eyes
These glasses make a useful addition to a mad professor's costume.

Spiral glued to clear acetate

Egg carton eyes   *Red frames*

Red, green, and gold glitter

Sequins

Rock star shades
Great for rock stars, these glasses are very glittery.

JEWEL BOX

You can add sparkle to any costume with these simple jewelry-making techniques. If you can't buy the gemstones shown below, make your own using silver, gold, or colored foil. Save the foil wrappers from chocolates and candies and you'll soon have all you need.

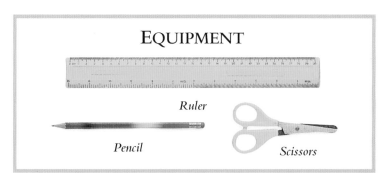

EQUIPMENT

Ruler

Pencil

Scissors

You will need

Corrugated cardboard

Gold and silver foil

Thick string

Gold cord★

Glue and a spatula

Flat-backed glass gemstones★

Thin wire for necklaces

Clear tape

Thin stick or dowel rod for wand

Making the jewels

1 Draw the jewelry shapes you want to make on corrugated cardboard using household objects as templates. Then cut them out.

2 For big jewels, such as a star for a wand or a medallion, cut out two large stars or circles and glue them together to make them stronger.

3 Spread glue over the shapes and stick pieces of string to them in circles or tight spirals. Set the shapes aside until the glue dries.

4 Cover each shape with foil, folding it to the back and gluing it down. Press the foil over the string so the pattern shows through.

5 Glue glass gemstones to the shapes for decoration. Use a large gem in the center of big shapes and glue smaller gems around the edges.

6 For a necklace, cut pieces of thin wire and bend them into loops. Tape a loop to the back of each jewel, then thread the loops onto some cord.

Glittering collection

You can use your jewels in lots of different ways: thread them onto braids or cords to make regal necklaces, belts, and medallions; glue them to earring or pin backs; or attach them to plain rings for a sparkling transformation.

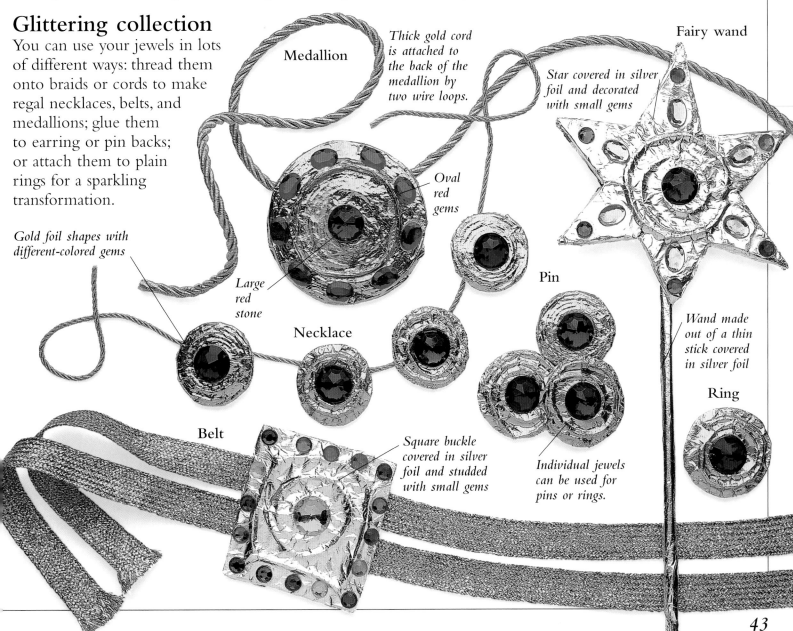

Medallion

Thick gold cord is attached to the back of the medallion by two wire loops.

Fairy wand

Star covered in silver foil and decorated with small gems

Oval red gems

Gold foil shapes with different-colored gems

Large red stone

Pin

Necklace

Wand made out of a thin stick covered in silver foil

Ring

Belt

Square buckle covered in silver foil and studded with small gems

Individual jewels can be used for pins or rings.

COSTUME PARADE

You have made masks, hats, cloaks, tunics, and full outfits. Here and on the next few pages you can see how simple accessories can complete an array of dazzling costumes.

Black gloves

Hat (page 14)

Cloak (page 28)

Wand

Long black T-shirt

Ghost costume (page 20)

Chain

Black tights

Black tights

Ghoulish ghost   Starry witch

Paper fringes tied around wrists and ankles

Orange pants and sweatshirt

Mask (page 6)

Mask (page 6)

Cape (page 28)

Feathered cape (page 28)

Mask (page 6)

Socks on hands

Pink T-shirt

Webbed feet cut out of yellow poster board and taped around ankles

Yellow tights

Green tights

Wild lion   Evil insect   Exotic bird

Costume
(page 18)

Shoulder guards
made from colored
poster board

Mustache
(page 38)

Hat
(page 14)

Jewels
(page 42)

Rock star
shades
(page 40)

Star-shaped
badge
(page 42)

Gold
shirt

Smart sheriff

Glamorous movie star

Leg guards
made in
same way
as gauntlets

Gauntlets
(see armor,
page 34)

Feet (see horse's
hooves, page 10)

Hat
(page 14)

Red foam
ball nose

Pop-out eyes
(page 40)

Hair
spiked
with gel

Ra-ra skirt
(page 26) worn
as neck ruff

Yellow
shirt

Space-age robot

Cheerful clown

Mad professor

Starry
headband
(page 14)

Devil costume
(page 36)

Bandaged head
(page 20)

Cape
(page 28)

Trident

Starry wand
(page 42)

Transparent cape
(page 28)

Tattered
clothes

Bandaged arm
and hand

Skirt
(page 26)

Red tights

Bandaged
feet

Good fairy

Fiendish devil

Horror mummy

COSTUME PARADE

*Costume
(page 10)*

*Mask and body
(page 10)*

*Hat and bendy
braids (page 38)*

T-shirt

Overalls

*Black poster-
board hooves*

Zippy zebra

*Basket of
carrots*

Wild stallion

Farm girl

*Matador hat
(page 16)
decorated with
skull and
crossbones*

*Paper flower
in hair*

*Wreath
(page 14)*

*Eye patch
(page 40)*

*Jewels
(page 42)*

*Paper garland
flowers*

*Sword
(page 32)*

*Toga
(page 23)*

*Grass skirt
(page 26)*

*Sarong
and top
(page 22)*

Hula-hula girl

Swashbuckling pirate

Desert island dancer

Roman emperor

Felt hat

Glasses
(page 40)

Mustache
(page 38)

Cotton
eyebrows
stuck to tape

Beard
(page 38)

Raincoat

Turban
(page 23)

Chocolate
coins

Chef's hat
(page 14)

Mustache
(page 38)

Undercover detective   **Busy fisherman**   **Rich sultan**   **Master chef**

Bow and arrow

Tunic
(page 24)

Dagger
(page 32)

Tall hat
(page 14)

Jeweled mask
(page 40)

Regal robe
(page 28)

Top hat
(page 14)

Cloak
(page 28)

Magic
scarf

Forest archer   **Medieval lady**   **Amazing magician**

Crown (page 14)

Shields and weapons
(page 32)

Body armor
(page 32)

Long T-shirt

Tunic
(page 24)

Leg guards
made in
same way as
gauntlets

Robe
(page 28)

Purple sash

Sword
(page 32)

Gold
poster-
board
buckles

Knights in armor   **Noble king**

47

INDEX

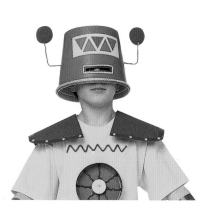